RESURRECTION -

31 MESSAGES

Our Future Resurrected Bodies

I0162852

LESLIE M. JOHN

This book of the law shall not depart out of thy mouth; but thou shalt meditate therein day and night, that thou mayest observe to do according to all that is written therein: for then thou shalt make thy way prosperous, and then thou shalt have good success. (Joshua 1:8)

Leslie M. John

Resurrection – 31 Messages

Leslie M. John

Resurrection – 31 Messages

Leslie M. John

RESURRECTION -

31 MESSAGES

Our Future Resurrected Bodies

My mission is to proclaim the good news of our Lord Jesus Christ as revealed to me through Holy Bible and from various teachers, preachers, and commentators. This is my voluntary service to God in the name of His only begotten Son Lord Jesus Christ.

Leslie M. John

I share the truth of knowledge of God with others with good intention of bringing them to the knowledge of the living God, the God of Abraham, the God of Isaac, the God of Jacob, and the Father of our Lord Jesus Christ. My mission is to proclaim the Gospel of Lord Jesus Christ and not converting forcibly any one to Christianity. One may accept or reject any or part of my writings/teachings.

These devotionals include excerpts from my book "David and Bathsheba"

All Scriptures are taken from KJV from open domain

ISBN-10: 0-9890283-4-8
ISBN-13: 978-0-9890283-4-9

Leslie M. John

Table of Contents

Leslie M. John

INTRODUCTION
GOD SPOKE TO JOSHUA

"This book of the law shall not depart out of thy mouth; but thou shalt meditate therein day and night, that thou mayest observe to do according to all that is written therein: for then thou shalt make thy way prosperous, and then thou shalt have good success". Joshua 1:8

Joshua spoke to the children of God, the Israelites, and advised them to be courageous and not to be afraid. Standing on the banks of Jordan River Joshua spoke at length to the children of Israel. Joshua was the successor of Moses in leadership to take them to the Promised Land Canaan.
"Be strong and of a good courage: for unto this people shalt thou divide for an inheritance the land, which I sware unto their fathers to give them". Joshua 1:6

"And they answered Joshua, saying, All that thou commandest us we will do, and whithersoever thou sendest us, we will go" (Joshua 1:16)

"For the preaching of the cross is to them that perish foolishness; but unto us which are saved it is the power of God" (1 Corinthians 1:18)

Leslie M. John

Apostle Paul writes that the message of the cross of Christ is foolishness to those, who are perishing, but to those who are saved it is the power of God. Paul preached the Gospel of Jesus and his crucifixion, but it was foolishness to Greeks. But the message of cross is power for those who believe in Jesus.

"For by one Spirit are we all baptized into one body, whether we be Jews or Gentiles, whether we be bond or free; and have been all made to drink into one Spirit". (1 Corinthians 12:13)

To the Jews the message of cross was not acceptable because they did not believe that Jesus bore our sins on the cross; rather they wanted to see signs and proofs. To the Greeks, who believed in philosophy and wisdom of this world, the message of cross was foolishness. Paul's main motto was to preach the gospel of Jesus. Speaking of Jesus he says...

"Who gave himself for our sins, that he might deliver us from this present evil world, according to the will of God and our Father" (Galatians 1:4)

Leslie M. John

DEVOTIONAL 1
GOD IS A SPIRIT

The answer to an intriguing question as to how does God look like is found in the the Gospel according to John Chapter 4 verse 24 which reads…"God is a Spirit: and they that worship him must worship him in spirit and in truth". Did anyone see God? God sent His only begotten Son into this world that whosoever believes in Him shall not perish but have everlasting life.

"For God so loved the world, that he gave his only begotten Son, that whosoever believeth in him should not perish, but have everlasting life". (John 3:16)

The very few verses from John's Gospel 1st Chapter present to us great Truth that "In the beginning was the Word, and the Word was with God, and the Word was God. The same was in the beginning with God.

All things were made by him; and wthout him was not anything made that was made. In him was life; and the life was the light of men". (John 1:1-4). The word became flesh.

It is so amazing that the Almighty God who created heaven and who cannot be contained in man-made buildings loved man so much that He sent His only begotten Son for our sake. God is a Spirit (John 4:24) and He went before the children of Israel by day in a pillar of a cloud and led them; and he went before them in a pillar of fire by night to give them light. (Exodus 13:21).

The LORD went before the children of Israel in a thick cloud in order that the people may hear when He speaks to Moses. (Exodus 19:9)

The LORD dwelt among them unseen by any one, yet performing miracles and helping them. In the Old Testament period God came and dwelt among the children of Israel and in the New Testament period the incarnate God humbled himself and dwelt among men in the form of man.

"And the LORD descended in the cloud, and stood with him there, and proclaimed the name of the LORD". (Exodus 34:5)

"And the Word was made flesh, and dwelt among us, (and we beheld his glory, the glory as of the only begotten of the Father,) full of grace and truth". (John 1:14)

"Who, being in the form of God, thought it not robbery to be equal with God: But made himself of no reputation, and took upon him the form of a servant, and was made in the likeness of men: And being found in fashion as a man, he humbled himself, and became obedient unto death, even the death of the cross " (Philippians 2:6-8)

Leslie M. John

Has anyone seen God?

"No man hath seen God at any time; the only begotten Son, which is in the bosom of the Father, he hath declared him" (John 1:18)

DEVOTIONAL 2
JESUS WAS BORN AS MAN

"For unto us a child is born, unto us a son is given: and the government shall be upon his shoulder: and his name shall be called Wonderful, Counsellor, The mighty God, The everlasting Father, The Prince of Peace" Isaiah 9:6

Seven hundred years before Christ, there lived a prophet called Isaiah. Isaiah 9:6 was a prophecy about Lord Jesus Christ.

Once upon a time there was a man sitting in the porch of his home watching birds at a distance. He threw some grains near him and waited to see if birds would come near to him. Birds slowly hopped, jumped and came near but not so near as to reach the grains because they feared if they came too near the man would harm them. The man realized that the birds were afraid and were, therefore, not coming near to him. The man, therefore, took the form of bird, and flew into their midst. The birds were happy and followed him to the grains and ate them. That was just a story.

When it comes to man he sinned and went far from God, who sent His only begotten Son, in the likeness of man to reconcile men unto the Father. The 'Son of God' became the 'Son of Man'.

Leslie M. John

In New Testament, Luke Chapter 1 verses 26 to 38 we read, "God sent the angel Gabriel to Nazareth, a town of Galilee, to a virgin pledged to be married to a man named Joseph, a descendent of David. The virgin's name was Mary.

The angel went to her and said, "Greetings, you who are highly favored! The Lord is with you." When Mary was afraid, the angel said, "Do not be afraid, Mary you have found favor with God. You will be with child and give birth to a son, and you are to give him the name Jesus. He will be great and will be called the Son of the Most High.

The Lord will give him the throne of David, and he will reign over the house of Jacob forever, his kingdom will never end.

"How this will be," Mary asked the angel, "since I am a virgin?"

The angel answered, "The Holy Spirit will come upon you, and the power of the Most High will overshadow you. So the holy one to be born will be called the Son of God."

Before Joseph and Mary came together, Mary was found with child through Holy Spirit. Because Joseph was a righteous man and did not want to expose her to public disgrace, he had in mind to put her away quietly. But after he had considered this, an angel of the Lord appeared to him in a dream and said, "Joseph son of David, do not be afraid to take

Mary home as your wife, because what is conceived in her is from the Holy Spirit. She will give birth to a son, and you are to give him the name Jesus, because he will save his people from their sins" (cf. Mt.1:18-24).

DEVOTIONAL 3
JESUS WAS FULLY DIVINE AND FULLY HUMAN

Prophet Isaiah's words were fulfilled. When Joseph woke up, he did what the angel of the Lord had commanded him and took Mary home as his wife. But he had no union with her until she gave birth to a son.

Jesus was born in a manger in Bethlehem. He grew up in a poor family, preached the Kingdom of God, Way to obtain salvation, died for our sake upon the cross of Calvary, was buried and rose upon the third day. Later, he ascended in to heaven

Jesus was called the "Son of Man". Jesus was fully divine and fully human when He was on this earth. His name was Jesus. He is Lord of all and He is the Christ, the Savior.

"God is not a man, that he should lie; neither the son of man, that he should repent: hath he said, and shall he not do [it]? or hath he spoken, and shall he not make it good?" Numbers 23:19

"But Jesus held his peace. And the high priest answered and said unto him, I adjure thee by the living God, that thou tell us whether thou be the Christ, the Son of God. Jesus saith unto him, Thou hast said: nevertheless I say unto you, Hereafter

Leslie M. John

16

shall ye see the Son of man sitting on the right hand of power, and coming in the clouds of heaven" Matthew 26:63,64 Salvation belongs to Him and Him alone and there is no salvation in any other.

"And Simon Peter answered and said, Thou art the Christ, the Son of the living God." Matthew 16:16

In the days when Lord Jesus was on this earth the people saw God in Jesus and yet did not know that He was God. He was fully divine and fully human.

Jesus grew up and taught the way to the Father. He said "I am the way, the truth, and the life: no man cometh unto the Father, but by me". He also said "If ye had known me, ye should have known my Father also: and from henceforth ye know him, and have seen him".

Then, Philip said to Lord Jesus to show the Father and Jesus said to him "Have I been so long time with you, and yet hast thou not known me, Philip? he that hath seen me hath seen the Father; and how sayest thou then, Shew us the Father?"

Lord Jesus was God in human form. He did miracles like giving sight to the blind, raising the dead. He said to them to believe that He was in the Father and Father in Him. (Cf. John 14:6-11)

Jesus was to die and before He died on the cross he said to the disciples that He will not leave them comfortless. He said that He would send the

Comforter, who was the Holy Spirit, whom the Father would send in His name and that Holy Spirit would teach them as also all of us all things and bring all things into remembrance. In our days we have Holy Spirit with us and in those who are born again. (Cf. John 14:18-21 and25-27)";

DEVOTIONAL 4
MOSES DESIRED TO SEE GOD

"And Moses said unto the LORD, See, thou sayest unto me, Bring up this people: and thou hast not let me know whom thou wilt send with me. Yet thou hast said, I know thee by name, and thou hast also found grace in my sight" (Exodus 33:12)

Moses finds a reason to plead with God and expresses his desire to see Him. The reason he quoted was that God said to him that He asked him to lead the people of Israel but did not tell him who will accompany him and yet he said that He knew Moses' name.

Moses desired to see God and prayed to Him to show Himself that Moses may know God fully well and know that Israel is His nation and the children of Israel are His people.

"Now therefore, I pray thee, if I have found grace in thy sight, shew me now thy way, that I may know thee, that I may find grace in thy sight: and consider that this nation is thy people" (Exodus 33:13)

God said to Moses that he found grace in the sight of Him and He knew Moses by his name. God said that He will make His goodness pass before Moses and will be gracious to him and show mercy on those whom He will have mercy. God also said to

Leslie M. John

Moses that he cannot see God's face because no man can see God and live after seeing His face.

God provided a solution to Moses that he should stand at a designated place upon a rock and when the glory of God passes by He shall place Moses in a cleft of the rock and cover him with His hand while He passes by.

After God passing by the place He would lift His hand and Moses could see His back parts but face shall not be seen (Exodus 33:17-23)

God had given to Moses two tablets containing the Ten Commandments as we read in Exodus Chapter 20 but then when he went down from the mount with the two tablets of the testimony, the work of God and the writing of God, in his hand he saw calf and the dancing.

Moses' anger waxed hot and he cast the tables out of his hand and broke them. (cf. Exodus 32:15-19). Moses saw God as detailed in Exodus 33:17-23 the LORD said to Moses to hew two tablets of stone like the first one "and the LORD descended in the cloud and stood with him there and proclaimed the name of the LORD" (Exodus 34:5)

Moses worshipped God and prayed that the LORD may go among the children of Israel. The LORD made covenant that He will drive out the Amorites, the Canaanites, the Hittites, Perizzites, the Hivite and the Jebusite.

Moses did not see God face to face because God is a Spirit and He had no physical body and God Himself said no one can see Him in His glory and live. Moses could hear the voice of the LORD.

DEVOTIONAL 5
HOW DID GOD SPEAK TO MAN?

"God, who at sundry times and in divers manners
spake in time past unto the fathers by the prophets,
Hath in these last days spoken unto us by his Son,
whom he hath appointed heir of all things, by whom
also he made the worlds; Who being the brightness
of his glory, and the express image of his person,
and upholding all things by the word of his power,
when he had by himself purged our sins, sat down
on the right hand of the Majesty on high" (Hebrews
1:1-3)

God spoke to Adam, Abraham, Moses and many
other prophets in the Old Testament period and to
many in the New Testament period and to many
after His resurrection and ascension.

From Genesis account it is clear that God had a
perfect relationship with Adam and He walked in
the cool of the day in the Garden of Eden.

Adam transgressed the commandment of God and
hid himself when God inquired of him as to where
he was. Adam said he was naked, and, therefore, he
hid from God.

Adam knew that he was naked only after he

transgressed the commandment of God. God
covered Adam with the skin of a dead animal by
removing the apron he made for himself with the
leaves by his own works. His works to cover his
nakedness was not enough in the sight of God and
He made His own provision for covering the
nakedness of Adam.

During this period much conversation took place
between God and Adam.

God expelled Adam and Eve from the Garden of
Eden in order that he may not lay hands on the tree
of life.

Man fell from the presence of God and man's
posterity could not see the glory of God from then
onwards until Lord Jesus Christ, who was with
Father, came into this world in the form of servant
in the likeness of man to redeem him from the
bondage of sin provided he repented of his sin and
to reconcile man with the Father. God spoke to
Moses from the burning bush.

"And when the LORD saw that he turned aside to
see, God called unto him out of the midst of the
bush, and said, Moses, Moses. And he said, Here
am I" Exodus 3:4

God spoke to Moses, His servant and Aaron, the
high priest from "Mercy Seat" in the Tabernacle.
God spoke to Abraham by coming in the form of
man. God spoke to prophets through visions and in

dreams. Lord Jesus was present with Shadrach, Meshach, and Abednego in fiery furnace (Christophany).

DEVOTIONAL 6
GOD SPOKE IN DIFFERENT WAYS

"And after the earthquake a fire; [but] the LORD [was] not in the fire: and after the fire a still small voice" 1 Kings 19:12

During the journey of Israelites in the wilderness God spoke to Moses several times. One such incidence is found in Exodus 19:16-19.

There were thunders and lightening and a thick cloud upon the Mount Sinai The trumpet sound was exceedingly loud and the people trembled.

While the people waited near the Mount Sinai God descended upon it in fire and some ascended as the smoke from a furnace. Mount Sinai was on a smoke and God responded to Moses in a voice.

In 1 Kings 18:20-40 there is a dramatic presentation of how Elijah proved that Jehovah is the real God, the God of heaven and earth, the God who created heavens, earth, seas and all that is therein. Baal and four hundred and fifty prophets of Baal were humiliated and Elijah killed them all.

The idol remained an idol speechless. God showed up on Mount Carmel in the form of fire and consumed the burnt sacrifice offered by Elijah.

Leslie M. John

25

Elijah was afraid of the threatening made by Jezebel, wife of wicked king, Ahab. She threatened to kill Elijah, and somehow Elijah's fear exceeded the success he had seen earlier. He went and hid in a cave where an angel of the Lord appeared to him and asked him to be courageous, rise and eat. Elijah obeyed and rose and ate for forty days and forty nights on the mount.

The LORD said to Elijah to stand upon the mount and Elijah did as the LORD said to him. God passed by and behold there was great and strong wind rent the mountains and broke the rocks but He was not there.

After this an earthquake took place and after earthquake a fire, but the LORD was not in the fire, but after the fire there God came to Elijah in a small still voice and spoke to him.

The word of the LORD came to Elijah and asked him "What doest thou here, Elijah?" Prophet Elijah answered the LORD God of hosts that he was very jealous for the LORD and while the children of Israel forsook the covenant, he was all alone left to stand for the LORD and his life is being sought after. God said to Elijah that there were He reserved seven thousand in Israel who did not bow their knees to Baal.

"Yet I have left [me] seven thousand in Israel, all the knees which have not bowed unto Baal, and every mouth which hath not kissed him" 1 Kings

19:18

In the following references we see that God spoke in fire, thunder, whirlwind besides speaking in still small voice.

Job 37:2 "Hear attentively the noise of his voice, and the sound [that] goeth out of his mouth"

Job 38:1 "Then the LORD answered Job out of the whirlwind, and said"

Psalm 104:7 "At thy rebuke they fled; at the voice of thy thunder they hasted away. Zechariah 4:6 Then he answered and spake unto me, saying, This [is] the word of the LORD unto Zerubbabel, saying, Not by might, nor by power, but by my spirit, saith the LORD of hosts"

John 12:29 "The people therefore, that stood by, and heard [it], said that it thundered: others said, An angel spake to him"

Revelation 4:5 "And out of the throne proceeded lightnings and thunderings and voices: and [there were] seven lamps of fire burning before the throne, which are the seven Spirits of God"

Thus we see that God spoke to man in different ways in different periods and the writer of Hebrews rightly said:

"God, who at sundry times and in divers manners

spake in time past unto the fathers by the prophets, Hath in these last days spoken unto us by [his] Son, whom he hath appointed heir of all things, by whom also he made the worlds" Hebrews 1:1-2 ";

DEVOTIONAL 7
GOD SPOKE BY HIS SON

"Hath in these last days spoken unto us by [his] Son, whom he hath appointed heir of all things, by whom also he made the worlds" Hebrews 1:2

Lord Jesus Christ spoke about the Father and said He and the Father are one and whoever has seen Him has seen the Father. The Son of God, Lord Jesus Christ, relinquished His glory in heaven, and came into this world. The Father, The Son, and The Holy Spirit are one and co-equal and co-existence. Lord Jesus Christ is the way, the truth and the life.

"I and my Father are one." John 10:30

"No man can come to me, except the Father which hath sent me draw him: and I will raise him up at the last day" John 6:44

"For he hath made him [to be] sin for us, who knew no sin; that we might be made the righteousness of God in him" 2 Corinthians 5:21

Lord Jesus Christ, the Son of God, became mediator between the Father and man to give man salvation. Lord Jesus Christ paid the price of redemption of man by taking upon Him the sin of man and dying

Leslie M. John

29

on the cross. His blood cleanses us from our sin provided we repent of our sins.

In the New Testament period before Jesus ascended into heaven he spoke in person face to face to some.

"Jesus saith unto her, Woman, why weepest thou? whom seekest thou? She, supposing him to be the gardener, saith unto him, Sir, if thou have borne him hence, tell me where thou hast laid him, and I will take him away" John 20:15

After Lord Jesus Christ is seated at the right hand of the Majesty Holy Spirit came into this world to be with His disciples and with all those who believed Him as Savior. The Holy Spirit dwelt in the believers as soon as they accepted Jesus as their Savior.

In the present age God speaks to us from His Holy Word and the Spirit who speaks strongly to us in our hearts convicting us the truth and providing way to escape from sinning.

God also speaks through preachers, teachers of the Word of God and sometimes also from the mouths of our closed ones, if they were believers in Lord Jesus Christ and had salvation.

In the kingdom age when Lord Jesus Christ comes He will speak to those who were justified as righteous during "Great Tribulation Period" and justified as righteous in the "Sheep and Goat judgment" in the same way as He spoke to His disciples and others after His resurrection from the dead. Every eye will see Lord Jesus Christ and acknowledge that He is Lord Jesus Christ, the Son of God, and the Savior.

"Behold, he cometh with clouds; and every eye shall see him, and they also which pierced him: and all kindreds of the earth shall wail because of him. Even so,Amen"(Revelation 1:7)";

DEVOTIONAL 8
MAN'S CURIOSITY

Man has an unflinching curiosity to know about the power of death, the death, and the life after death. There are many myths about the death and even among Christians there are differing views.

Bible gives a believer in Christ great comfort that he or she will be with the Lord for ever and ever after death. The life after death is extremely pleasant and good according to Scriptures and, therefore, a believer in Christ does not need to be afraid of death.

Lord Jesus Christ defeated the power of death and the death once and for all by His own resurrection. The grave could not hold Him and He resurrected without seeing any corruption of His body.

Jesus said He had the power to lay down His life and take it back at his own discretion and He did so. Lord Jesus Christ also assured his followers that they need not be afraid of death because He gives them everlasting life.

According to Bible Lord Jesus Christ is the only one who has the authority to pardon sins of a person, and salvation is by grace through faith in Him. Jesus is the Son of God, and the very God Himself. Jesus became one like us and came to this

Leslie M. John

earth, lived like a man among us. Jesus was fully divine and fully human and this truth is very hard to understand by an unbeliever.

Jesus died, rose on the third day and ascended into heaven. He is seated at the right hand of the Father highly exalted. He is given the name above all names and every knee shall bow to Him. Jesus will come again soon.

The Scripture says that we shall not all sleep, but we shall all be changed. When Lazarus was dead for four days Jesus saw him and said "Our friend Lazarus sleepeth…" The disciples of Jesus took his saying at face value and thought Lazarus was, indeed, sleeping.

However, Jesus spoke of the death of Lazarus and said he is dead. Jesus said that He will wake him up from his sleep, indicating that He will raise Lazarus. Martha believed and said to Jesus that she knew Lazarus would rise in the resurrection at the last day. But then, Jesus said He is the resurrection.(Cf. John: 11:13, 14, 24 ,25)

"Jesus said unto her, I am the resurrection, and the life: he that believeth in me, though he were dead, yet shall he live" (John 11:25)";

DEVOTIONAL 9
MARY DID NOT RECOGNIZE JESUS

It is interesting that the Peter and John disciples of Lord Jesus Christ did not take it serious that there was scripture saying that He will rise again. Mary Magdalene did not recognize Lord Jesus Christ until He called her by name.

"And said unto them, Thus it is written, and thus it behoved Christ to suffer, and to rise from the dead the third day" (Luke 24:46)

The narration of the resurrection of our Lord Jesus Christ is marvelously described in John Chapter 20.

On the first day of the week Mary Magdalene went to the sepulcher and saw that stone was taken away from the sepulcher. She was surprised to see that there was no stone laid on the sepulcher.

Before Jesus was buried the chief priests and Pharisees went to Pilate and said to him that Jesus had told that He will rise again in three days, and, therefore, a command be issued that the sepulcher be secured well until the third day, in order that the disciples of Jesus may not go and steal the body and say that He rose from the dead. Pilate agreed to their suggestion and said to them to have watch and make it secure as they can.

Leslie M. John

The chief priests and Pharisees, therefore, went and made sure that the sepulcher was secured with the seal on the stone and setting a watch. (cf. Matthew 27:62-66)

From Matthew 15:47 and Matthew 27:56 it can be seen there Mary Magdalene, was not the Mary the mother of Jesus. There were several women by the name "Mary" but here the name of Mary Magdalene is mentioned. Mary Magdalene was the woman out of whom seven devils were cast out and she was healed of evil spirits and infirmities.

And certain women, which had been healed of evil spirits and infirmities, Mary called Magdalene, out of whom went seven devils, (Luke 8:2)

Mary Magdalene ran to Simon Peter, and the other disciple (John), whom Jesus loved, and said to them that "they have taken away the Lord out of the sepulcher and we not where they have laid Him".

Mary Magdalene was the first to reach the sepulcher but there were other women also with her. Other women were Mary the mother of James, and Salome. (Cf. Mark 16:1 and Matthew 28:1)

Peter and John ran to the sepulcher but John outran Peter and reached the Sepulcher. John stooped down and looked in and saw linen clothes lying but he did not go in. Peter came following came in and went into the sepulcher and saw that linen lie there. Importantly the napkin that was wrapped around the body of Lord Jesus was not along with the linen clothes but it was found wrapped together in a place by itself.

From John 11:44 it is understood that there was napkin around the face of Lazarus whom Lord Jesus resurrected. Here we see the napkin was not along with linen but it was found in a place by itself. Then John also went into the sepulcher and saw and believed they Lord Jesus Christ rose from the dead.

Surprisingly, even though they were disciple of Lord Jesus Christ they did not know that there was scripture saying that he must rise again from the dead. There were two scriptures according to which Lord Jesus Christ should rise from the dead.

"Ought not Christ to have suffered these things, and to enter into his glory?" (Luke 24:26)

"And said unto them, Thus it is written, and thus it behoved Christ to suffer, and to rise from the dead the third day" (Luke 24:46)

DEVOTIONAL 10
CHRIST'S BODY AFTER RESURRECTION

"For as yet they knew not the scripture, that he must rise again from the dead. Then the disciples went away again unto their own home" (John 20:9-10)

The disciples of Lord Jesus Christ went home but Mary stood outside the sepulcher and wept. She stooped down and looked into the sepulcher and saw two angels in white sitting. One angel was sat at the head and the other at feet where the body of Lord Jesus Christ was laid.

The angels inquired Mary as to why she was weeping and she said to the angels that they have taken away Her Lord, and she did not know where they have laid Him. Immediately she turned back and saw Lord Jesus Christ standing but she did not recognize Him. She thought she saw gardener and asked Him if He had taken away the body of Lord Jesus Christ, and if so, she would take the body away.

Lord Jesus Christ called her by name and Mary recognized Him and called Him as "Master"

Mary Magdalene recognized Lord Jesus Christ only after He called her by name. She responded by saying "Rabboni" which is to say "Master". The Lord said to her not to touch her because He did not ascend unto the Father. There are some interpretations contradictory to each other about Lord Jesus Christ asking her not to touch Him.

The simplest explanation is that she should not cling to her as an obstruction to Him nor she should stop at that but to go ahead and tell His disciples about His resurrection and that He will ascend unto the Father.

Mary Magdalene went to the disciples of Lord Jesus Christ and told them that she saw Lord Jesus Christ and about the instructions the Lord gave to her. It was the first day of the week and on the same evening the disciples assembled with the doors shut because they feared Jews.

Lord Jesus Christ came into their midst even when the doors remain shut and said to them "Peace be unto you". After this He showed His hands which were nailed and His body which was scourged. The disciples saw Lord Jesus Christ and were glad. Lord Jesus Christ said to them once again "Peace be unto you"

DEVOTIONAL 11
LORD JESUS APPEARD TO THOMAS

Lord Jesus Christ commissioned them to proclaim the Gospel and said to them just as the Father sent Him with a mission He was also sending His disciples with a mission and He breathed on them saying "Receive ye the Holy Ghost".

Later in Acts Chapter 1 it is recorded that that they should wait at Jerusalem and they should start on their mission only after the Holy Ghost had come upon them.

No one except God only can forgive any one's sins and there should not be any misunderstanding about Lord saying to them that whosoever sins they remit they are remitted and whosoever sins they retain shall be retained.

Each individual is responsible for his/her own sins and only when they repent of their sins they receive salvation. Lord Jesus Christ's words were in relation to the building of the Church.

Thomas Didymus was not with them when Lord Jesus Christ appeared to the disciples when the doors were shut and He breathed on them the Holy Spirit. When other disciples said to them they saw the Lord Thomas said to them that unless he sees Lord Jesus Christ personally and see in his hands nail marks and put his finger into the print marks of the nails and his side he would not believe. After eight days again when the disciples were in closed doors Thomas was also with them.

Lord Jesus Christ came into their midst, even the second time, when the doors were shut and said "Peace be unto you".

Lord Jesus Christ said to Thomas to put his finger into His hands and His side to make sure that He was Lord Jesus Christ and also admonished him that he should not be faithless but be a believer in Him.

Thomas answered and said "My Lord and my God". Lord Jesus Christ did many miracles and they are not all recorded, but only those which are enough to prove that He was the Son of God and by believing they may have life through His name.

"I will declare the decree: the LORD hath said unto me, Thou art my Son; this day have I begotten thee" (Psalms 2:7)

"Therefore my heart is glad, and my glory rejoiceth: my flesh also shall rest in hope. For thou wilt not leave my soul in hell; neither wilt thou suffer thine Holy One to see corruption" (Psalms 16:9-10)

DEVOTIONAL 12
THE LORD IS ALWAYS WITH US

"Go ye therefore, and teach all nations, baptizing them in the name of the Father, and of the Son, and of the Holy Ghost: Teaching them to observe all things whatsoever I have commanded you: and, lo, I am with you alway, [even] unto the end of the world. Amen" (Matthew 28:19-20)

Thomas Didymus, who was one of the disciples of Lord Jesus Christ, was not present along with the other disciples when they assembled together at one place because of the fear of Jews.

When Lord Jesus Christ appeared to them even when the doors were shut He removed their fear from them and said unto them "Peace be unto you".

The Lord gave His peace to them. His peace was not as the world gave but it was that peace soothes the hearts of those who receive it and it is everlasting. The peace that the Lord gives to us infuses courage in us who trust Him as the Lord.

It was at a different time period when the disciples told Thomas that they saw the Lord. The conversation among the disciples of Lord Jesus Christ is interesting. The disciples of Lord Jesus Christ who saw Him gave testimony that they saw Him, but Thomas was not convinced with their testimony and surely desired to see Him and believe that He is the Lord. He desired to place finger in the print marks of the nails in the hands of Jesus Christ and thrust his hands into the side of the Lord.

It was after eight days when all the disciples and this time including Thomas assembled together Lord Jesus Christ appeared to them second time and said to them "Peace be unto you".

It is very noteworthy that Thomas did not ask Lord Jesus Christ directly to show His hands in order that he may thrust his finger into the nail-marks in His hands and thrust his hand into the side of the Lord, but it was Lord Jesus Christ, who voluntarily offered to show to Thomas Didymus and called him by his name.

The Lord said to him that he may do what he desired to do to be sure of the fact that he saw the Lord.

Obviously the disciples did not know that the Lord heard the disciples when they spoke to Thomas that they saw the Lord. Their testimony about Lord Jesus Christ was not in the same place where they assembled earlier but it was outside the place. Thomas was not present when they assembled earlier and now he was with them when the disciples gave testimony about the Lord.

With all the disciples including Thomas Didymus assembled the Lord appeared to them again and said to them second time "Peace be unto you". It was this time that the Lord Himself said to Thomas to put his finger into His hands and His side that he may believe that He was the Lord.

It was even before Thomas asked the Lord to show his hands and his side that the Lord Himself offered his hands and side to Thomas to peruse and believe.

The Lord was with them first time and until he said "Peace be unto you" they did not recognize Him. Thomas did not recognize the Lord until he placed his fingers into the nail-marks of Lord Jesus and thrust his hand into His side.

The Lord was with all of them when they were conversing with one another outside but they did not see the Lord. The Lord heard their conversation but they knew not that the Lord heard them speak to one another. The Lord offered voluntarily to Thomas His hands and side to be perused that he may believe that He was their Lord and Savior. Thomas believed and called out loudly "My Lord and my God".

The Lord is always with us even if we do not see Him physically.

Leslie M. John

DEVOTIONAL 13
RESURRECTED BODY

"And he said unto them, Cast the net on the right side of the ship, and ye shall find. They cast therefore, and now they were not able to draw it for the multitude of fishes" (John 21:6)

After Thomas was convinced of his question about resurrection of Lord Jesus Christ Jesus showed Himself again to the disciples at the sea of Tiberias. His appearance was not before Simon Peter and Thomas, Nathanael and sons of Zebedee and two other disciples decided to turn to their own professions because they were still unsure about the resurrection of Lord Jesus Christ.

It all appeared, perhaps, as fable to them that in spite of seeing Lord Jesus Christ little while ago they decided to return to their own professions.

Simon Peter said "I go a fishing" and the rest of the disciples concurred with him and said that they also will follow him. As they turned to their profession according to their own choice and will they caught not even a single fish the entire night even though they were professional fishers.

Early in the morning desperate as they were with no

yield Lord Jesus stood on the shore and yet the disciples did not recognize Him. It is strange that even though the Lord appeared to them little while ago to Peter and other disciples except Thomas when they were assembled even when the doors were shut and said to them "Peace be unto you" and then later when Thomas was present in their midst after eight days Jesus appeared to them even when the doors were shut and yet they did not recognize Him this time at the shore.

Lord Jesus Christ asked them "Children have ye any meat?" and they answered "No". Jesus said to them to cast the net on the right side of the ship and assured them they shall find the fish.

They took His suggestion and cast their net on the right side of their ship and the catch was so great that they could not draw the net out because of the multitude of the fishes in the net.

At this point John recognized Lord Jesus Christ and said to Simon Peter that it was Lord Jesus Christ who stood on the shore and asked them to cast the net on the right side of the ship. Simon Peter heard from John about Lord Jesus Christ and he jumped into the sea after girding himself with fisher's coat because he was naked until then. The simplicity of Peter is adorable; nonetheless he was quick in actions.

Simon Peter was a fisherman who followed Lord Jesus Christ from the time he was called and yet he did not recognize the risen Lord Jesus Christ. He thought of walking on water when he saw Jesus walking on water because he stumbled in faith he started sinking. But when he called out to Lord Jesus Christ in faith to save him, the Lord responded immediately and pulled him out of the water to safety.

When Jesus was about to be crucified he said, inadvertently, such a thing may not happen to him but the Lord said to him to get behind him because he was harboring evil thoughts.

The purpose of Jesus coming into this world was to fulfill the will of the Father and to bruised for our sins and Peter did not know that purpose.

Peter pulled out his sword and cut the ear of one of the soldiers when they were arresting Jesus but the Lord said to him that he who strives to live by the sword will die by the sword and he healed the soldier with restoring his ear.

Peter denied Jesus three times but repented later. In his life Simon Peter stood as a great testimony for Lord Jesus Christ and history says that he was crucified upside down according to his voluntary disposition in consequence of the persecution he faced for standing for Him.

Jesus was crucified on the cross and was buried and he rose from the dead with uncorrupted body in His glorified body on the third day.

Leslie M. John

It is so comforting to note that we will also rise with glorified bodies at the resurrection when out Lord Jesus Christ returns.

"But some man will say, How are the dead raised up? and with what body do they come? Thou fool, that which thou sowest is not quickened, except it die: And that which thou sowest, thou sowest not that body that shall be, but bare grain, it may chance of wheat, or of some other grain" (1 Corinthians 15:35-37)

DEVOTIONAL 14
THE TWO SAW JESUS AT EMMAUS

"Therefore doth my Father love me, because I lay down my life, that I might take it again. No man taketh it from me, but I lay it down of myself. I have power to lay it down, and I have power to take it again. This commandment have I received of my Father" (John 10:17-18)

Although the names of the two are not revealed it is evident from the context that these two were disciples of Lord Jesus Christ. One of the disciples was Cleopatus and another is believed by some as Peter and some as Luke.

As they walked down the road on the day of resurrection of Lord Jesus in a village called Emmaus they communed with each other about the trial of Jesus, His crucifixion, His death and burial. As they reasoned about these things that happened in Jerusalem Jesus came near them and walked with them. He inquired them of what things they were talking about.

Even though they were the disciples of Lord Jesus Christ and saw resurrected Jesus with them they did not recognize Him.

Leslie M. John

Cleopas answered and asked Jesus a counter question if He was stranger in that land! His question was to ask how that He did not know the recent burning issues that have just happened three days ago. Jesus asked Cleopas as to what things have happened there.

The question from Jesus was not because He did not know what has happened recently there but to get more information about their knowledge about the things that have come to pass. Surprisingly, Cleopas gave reply that the things he was talking about were about Jesus of Nazareth who was a prophet mighty in deeds and word before God and all the people.

Jesus said the Father loves Him because He lays down His life that He might take it again. No one can take His life from Him, but He lays it down of Himself and He has the power to lay it down and He has the power to take it again.

Cleopas said that Jesus was to restore the kingdom to Israel and redeem them but the chief Priests and the rulers delivered Jesus to be condemned to death and have crucified Him. He also said that it was the third day after these things have happened. He also explained to Jesus how that certain women went to sepulcher that morning and astonished not finding the body of Jesus in the open sepulcher. The women went out then to give testimony how that the angels told them that Jesus was alive but they did not see Him.

Leslie M. John

The two disciples did not recognize Jesus until He revealed Himself by breaking bread at evening meal.

"And it came to pass, as he sat at meat with them, he took bread, and blessed it, and brake, and gave to them. And their eyes were opened, and they knew him; and he vanished out of their sight" (Luke 24:30-31) ";

DEVOTIONAL 15
THE TESTIMONY OF JESUS IS THE SPIRIT OF PROPHECY

"...O fools, and slow of heart to believe all that the prophets have spoken: Ought not Christ to have suffered these things, and to enter into his glory? And beginning at Moses and all the prophets, he expounded unto them in all the scriptures the things concerning himself" (Luke 24:25-27)

The Scriptures Lord Jesus was referring to were:

Genesis 3:15; 49:10; Numbers 21:8-9; Deuteronomy 18:15; Isaiah 9:6-7; 53:1-12; Psalm 16:1-11,1-11,1-7; Daniel 9:25-27; Malachi 4:2-6.

In spite of all these the two disciples did not recognize Lord Jesus Christ and as they were nearing the village He made as though He would have gone further, but they constrained Him to stay with them because it was already evening.

Lord Jesus Christ accepted their invitation and stayed with them and as they sat for evening meal He took bread and blessed it, and broke it and gave to them. It was then that their eyes were opened and Lord Jesus Christ vanished from that place.

The two disciples discerned then that the one who spoke to them all the while on the road and sat with them for evening meal was Lord Jesus Christ. They believed that Lord Jesus Christ rose from the dead and gave testimony about Him. (cf. Luke 24:13-15)

Lord Jesus Christ was recognized only when He revealed Himself and when He broke the bread and gave it them to eat. They believed and stood to testify Him.

"And I fell at his feet to worship him. And he said unto me, See thou do it not: I am thy fellow-servant, and of thy brethren that have the testimony of Jesus: worship God: for the testimony of Jesus is the spirit of prophecy" (Revelation 19:10)

DEVOTIONAL 16
THE LORD ATE FISH

"And they gave him a piece of a broiled fish, and of an honeycomb. And he took [it], and did eat before them". Luke 24:42-43

After Lord Jesus disappearing from the midst of the two disciples to whom he revealed that He was the risen Christ the two disciples testified in Jerusalem about the risen Lord Jesus Christ. As they spoke about Jesus Christ He appeared and stood in the midst of them.

It may be noted that in all these appearances of Lord Jesus Christ His appearances were sudden, and disappearances were sudden. They did not recognize Lord Jesus Christ until He Himself revealed to them in one way or the other. He also wished "Peace be unto you" in certain cases.

In this instance as the two disciples testified about risen Lord, the Lord Himself appeared to them and stood in their midst and said to them "Peace be unto you". When they saw Lord Jesus Christ they did not recognize Him, but rather they were afraid and thought that they saw a spirit.

Comforting as He was, our Lord Jesus Christ

Leslie M. John

questioned the disciples and others who assembled there as to why there were troubled in their minds and why do doubts arise in their minds about the Lord. He questioned them as to whether or not they remember the prophecies which spoke about Him and His crucifixion, burial and resurrection.

Just before questioning them about their remembering of the prophecies He showed evidence that He was indeed Lord Jesus Christ. He said to them to have a close look at his hands and feet and also touch Him and see because a spirit does not have flesh and bones.

Jesus said to them that because they could see Him, the nail marks on His hands and feet, they should believe that He was the risen Christ.

Going little more in His conversation with them the Lord asked them if they had any meat to eat. The Lord decided to show more proof of His resurrection because even after seeing Him physically and seeing the nail marks on His hands and feet they did not believe He was the Lord Jesus Christ. They gave Lord Jesus Christ a piece of broiled fish and of a honeycomb and He took it and ate before them.

Lord Jesus Christ said to them that the words that He spoke to them while He was with them were the fulfillment of the prophecies as written in the Law of Moses and in the prophetical books, in Psalms concerning Him. It was then that their eyes were open and they understood the scriptures.

The Lord reveals Himself to those whom He wish to and their eyes open to see Him and the Scriptures about Him only when He opens Himself to men who decide to follow Him with zeal.

The Lord reiterated that it is written in the prophecies that He was to come, die for our sake, and rise from the dead on the third day and also that repentance and must be preached in His name in all the nations beginning at Jerusalem because they were the live witnesses of Him. He said to them He will send the promise of the Father upon them as they tarry in the city of Jerusalem.

It is they who were supposed to wait for the Holy Spirit and the place where they were to wait was Jerusalem. There is no command for the Church to wait for the Holy Spirit to come upon them either at Jerusalem or at any place.

We are privileged that we receive Holy Spirit immediately at the time of our repentance of our sins to Lord Jesus Christ and accept Him as our savior. Lord Jesus Christ led them until they reached Bethany and parted from them after blessing them. The commandment to preach the Gospel can also be seen in Acts 1:8.

Indeed they worshipped Lord Jesus Christ and returned to Jerusalem with great joy and after that they continually praised God.

Leslie M. John

55

"But ye shall receive power, after that the Holy Ghost is come upon you: and ye shall be witnesses unto me both in Jerusalem, and in all Judaea, and in Samaria, and unto the uttermost part of the earth" Acts 1:8";

DEVOTIONAL 17
OUR BODIES AT RESURRECTION

"Thou fool, that which thou sowest is not quickened, except it die" 1 Corinthians 15:36

Concerning the resurrection and resurrected body Apostle Paul explains in 1 Corinthians 15:35-58 There would be many questions as to how the dead are raised and what their bodies look like when they are raised from the dead. A seed that is sown in the ground should die first before it comes up with a quickened body.

The seed sown in the ground, whether it be of wheat or some other grain, is not sown as a full-grown body but it is sown as a seed. It is God who gives the seed a body that pleases Him and every seed comes up with a different body that God gives it.

A butterfly before it has undergone metamorphosis would be like a worm but when it becomes a butterfly it is so beautiful. The flesh of man differs from that of the flesh of animals, fish and birds. Some bodies are terrestrial, and some celestial and these differ from one another.

God has also placed celestial bodies in the galaxy.

Leslie M. John

The Sun, the moon, the stars differ from one another and each star differs in glory from the other.

So is the resurrected body of the dead. The body is sown in corruption, dishonor, weakness but when it is raised it is raised in incorruption, glory, and in power.

The natural body dies and is raised in spiritual body. The resurrected body has the likeness of natural body and spiritual body similar to the one of risen Lord, who could suddenly appear and disappear at a place where He desired to go and even passing the shut doors and also could eat fish.

DEVOTIONAL 18
WE WILL BE CAUGHT UP AND WILL BE LIKE HIM

"For the Lord himself shall descend from heaven with a shout, with the voice of the archangel, and with the trump of God: and the dead in Christ shall rise first: Then we which are alive [and] remain shall be caught up together with them in the clouds, to meet the Lord in the air: and so shall we ever be with the Lord" 1 Thessalonians 4:16-17

The first man Adam was made a living soul when God breathed His spirit into his nostrils and the last Adam, who is our Lord Jesus Christ, became a quickening spirit. The first man was not spiritual but had a fleshly natural body but the resurrected body is spiritual.

God created man in His own image in the likeness of the triune God. (Genesis 1:26-27).

God created man out of dust and man returns to dust when he dies. The death came into this world as a result of sin and Lord Jesus Christ was triumphant over death. Man belongs to earth but Lord Jesus Christ was from heaven. The body which is created from the earth belongs to earth and the body that is from heaven belongs to heaven. Flesh

Leslie M. John

59

and blood cannot inherit the kingdom of God. The natural body needs to necessarily die to acquire heavenly body. Corrupted body cannot inherit incorruption. The resurrection and resurrected body was a mystery for long but is revealed unto us.

We have a fair idea about the attributes of resurrected body and we will have a change in the twinkling of an eye at the last trump when Lord Jesus Christ comes in clouds with the shout of an archangel and we are caught up to meet Him in the air to be with Him for ever and ever.

"Beloved, now are we the sons of God, and it doth not yet appear what we shall be: but we know that, when he shall appear, we shall be like him; for we shall see him as he is. And every man that hath this hope in him purifieth himself, even as he is pure" (1 John 3:2-3)

DEVOTIONAL 19
WE SHALL REIGN WITH HIM

It pleased the Father to bruise the Son on the Cross for our sake in order that we may be saved from destruction. Jesus died for our sake and bore our sins in order that whosoever believes in Him shall not perish but have everlasting life.

Jesus, who knew no sin, was made sin for us that we might be made righteousness of God in Him. All those who have received salvation by believing in Lord Jesus Christ as their Savior are the members of the Church, the body of Christ. The body is the Church and the head is Lord Jesus Christ. All those who are saved are baptized into one body

"whether we be Jews or Gentiles, whether we be bond or free; and have been all made to drink into one Spirit". Irrespective of man's clan or lineage the only thing that matters is whether or not a person has accepted Lord Jesus Christ as his/her personal savior. All those who are saved by the precious blood of Christ are equal.

This mystery was revealed in the New Testament as recorded in Ephesians 3:6 that Gentiles are given the privilege to be equal with Jews provided they confess their sins and accept Lord Jesus Christ as

Leslie M. John

their Savior.

When the Lord Himself descends from heaven with a shout with the voice of the archangel, and with the trump of God, the dead in Christ will rise fist and then those who are alive and remain will be caught up together with them in the clouds to meet Him in the air. All those who are saved will be with the Lord for ever and ever but those who have not received salvation will be left behind on this earth. There will be Jews and there will be Gentiles among the left-behind.

Those who are caught up to meet the Lord in the clouds will be with the transformed and glorified bodies. This transformation occurs in the twinkling of an eye. But those who are on the earth will still be in the earthly corruptible body.

The Church, the bride of Christ and also the body of Christ consisting of those who are caught up into the clouds to meet the Lord in the air will reign for ever and ever. Angel Gabriel appeared to Mary and said that she shall conceive in her womb and bring forth a Son, and His name shall be JESUS.

"...He shall be great, and shall be called the Son of the Highest: and the Lord God shall give unto him the throne of his father David" (Luke 1:31-32) The prophecy in Luke 1:33 that "...he shall reign over the house of Jacob forever; and of his kingdom there shall be no end" will be fulfilled in

Leslie M. John

the thousand year reign of Lord Jesus Christ and those who blessed and saved and caught up to be with the Lord shall be priests of God and of Christ and shall reign with Him.

"Blessed and holy is he that hath part in the first resurrection: on such the second death hath no power, but they shall be priests of God and of Christ, and shall reign with him a thousand years". (Revelation 20:6) (Ref. 1 Corinthians 12:13, 2 Corinthians 5:21, Ephesians 3:6, 1 Thessalonians 4:16-17)

DEVOTIONAL 20
THE SECOND COMING

"In my Father's house are many mansions: if it were not so, I would have told you. I go to prepare a place for you" (John 14:2).
The second coming of Lord Jesus is imminent. For a believer, rapture is the second coming of Jesus and for an unbeliever the second appearance of Jesus on the earth is the second coming of Jesus.

The end times prophecies are detailed for us in order that we may have faith and blessed hope of being received by Lord Jesus Christ and be with Him eternally.

The sequence of events leading to the Second coming of Jesus and his establishment of the millennial rule on the earth is disputed among Christians. However the undisputable fact is that the return of the Lord Jesus Christ and the resurrection of the dead saints from their graves followed by the living saints will be caught up is true.

The Pre-tribulation believes that the Church will not face the 'great tribulation' under Antichrist, while the Post-tribulation believes that the Church

Leslie M. John

will face the 'great tribulation' under Antichrist, but will be protected by God. The doctrine of 'Rapture' of the Church for keeping it away from the 'great tribulation' in the midair for seven years is as disputed as the doctrine of rapture of the Church after the 'great tribulation'.

The word, 'rapture's is not found in the Scriptures; however in essence the meaning of the said word is getting caught up into the air. The rapture dealing with the believers getting caught up to meet the Lord in the clouds is undisputed among both the groups.

Lord Jesus Christ's purpose of coming again to this earth is two-fold; firstly the second coming is for receiving His own to Himself and secondly, to fulfill the promises made to Israel. Church consisting of saved ones constitutes His bride and the marriage of the bride takes place according to Scriptures after the Church is caught up in the clouds, to meet the Lord in the air.

To this marriage between the Lord and His bride are not invited the unsaved ones. Lord Jesus Christ promised mansions for His Children, who believe in Him.

Jesus promised that He was going to heaven to prepare mansions for them. This promise is given in John 14:2 and 3 and this purpose, which was a

Leslie M. John

mystery in the Old Testament, is revealed in the New Testament. The earthly blessings promised to the children of Israel will be restored unto them when Lord Jesus Christ appears on this earth, while the heavenly blessings promised to His bride are given after the Church is caught up in the clouds to meet the Lord in the air.

DEVOTIONAL 21
SHEEP AND GOAT JUDGMENT

"The LORD said unto my Lord, Sit thou at my right hand, until I make thine enemies thy footstool" (Psalms 110:1)

After the seventieth week of prophesy as mentioned in Daniel 9:24 is fulfilled Lord Jesus Christ, with his bride i.e the Church, will step on the Mount of Olives. This is the Second Advent of Lord Jesus Christ on this earth. The First Advent was when Jesus was born in Bethlehem in a Manger (Luke 2:7,12 and 16).

Lord Jesus Christ with the resurrected saints will step on the Mount of Olives which is before Jerusalem on the east side. He returns to this earth with the armies of heaven as described in Revelation 19:14. It says:

"And the armies which were in heaven followed him upon white horses, clothed in fine linen, white and clean"

When the feet of Lord Jesus Christ touch the Mount of Olives it will cleave in the midst thereof toward the east and toward the west, and there shall be a very great valley; and half of the

Leslie M. John

mountain shall remove toward the north and half of it toward the south.

The people who persecuted Jesus will try to flee through this valley. This valley is called "Valley of Jehoshaphat" (Joel 3:1-2). There was neither a valley nor is now a valley by the name of "Valley of Jehoshaphat" but this is future event.

The meaning of the phrase "Valley of Jehoshaphat" is "The Lord Judges". This is the throne of Lord Jesus from where he judges the nations of this earth. This judgement is not Great White Throne judgment, but it is the judgement of what is described as "Sheep and Goat Judgment" as we read in Matthew 25:33-46

DEVOTIONAL 22
STANDING ON THE MOUNT OF OLIVES

Zechariah 14:4 "And his feet shall stand in that day upon the mount of Olives, which is before Jerusalem on the east, and the mount of Olives shall cleave in the midst thereof toward the east and toward the west, and there shall be a very great valley; and half of the mountain shall remove toward the north, and half of it toward the south". 1 Thessalonians 4:17 "Then we which are alive and remain shall be caught up together with them in the clouds, to meet the Lord in the air: and so shall we ever be with the Lord".

These prophecies tell us that Jesus will be on the earth and rule from Jerusalem from the throne of David. These two prophecies from Zechariah 14:4 and 1 Thessalonians 4:17 show us that Jesus will descend from heaven and after the seventieth week of Daniel's prophecy is completed He will step on Mount of Olives. He will judge nations and then rule from the throne of David for one thousand years. Jesus is waiting until all His enemies are brought to His footstool.

It is quite relevant here to meditate on the Psalm of David, where David prophesied the LORD (that is the Father) said to the Lord (that is The Son, Lord Jesus) to sit at His right hand, until He makes all His enemies his footstool.

"The LORD said unto my Lord, Sit thou at my right hand, until I make thine enemies thy footstool" (Psalms 110:1)

After the seventieth week of prophesy as mentioned in Daniel 9:24 is fulfilled Lord Jesus Christ, with his bride i.e. the Church, will step on the Mount of Olives. This is the Second Advent of Lord Jesus Christ on this earth.

The First Advent was when Jesus was born in Bethlehem in a Manger (Luke 2:7, 12 and 16). Lord Jesus Christ with the resurrected saints will step on the Mount of Olives which is before Jerusalem on the east side. He returns to this earth with the armies of heaven as described in Revelation 19:14. It says:

"And the armies which were in heaven followed him upon white horses, clothed in fine linen, white and clean"

There was neither a valley nor is now a valley by the name of "Valley of Jehoshaphat" but this is future event. The meaning of the phrase "Valley of Jehoshaphat" is "The Lord Judges".

Leslie M. John

This is the throne of Lord Jesus from where he judges the nations of this earth. This judgment is not Great White Throne judgment, but it is the judgment of what is described as "Sheep and Goat Judgment" as we read in Matthew 25:33-46.

DEVOTIONAL 23
JUDGMENT OF NATIONS
(ALSO KNOWN AS 'SHEEP AND GOAT JUDGMENT')

The judgment of nations is distinct from the 'Great White Throne Judgment. The nations are the living ones that survive through the 'great tribulation' period, when the gentiles, who are left-behind, are judged. This is a period after the Church consisting of believers is 'caught up' to be with the Lord for ever and ever.

In Matthew 5:31-46 there is a description of the judgment that takes place after Lord Jesus Christ reveals himself at His second coming to every one upon this earth. These are the ones, who missed the blessings of being 'caught up' to be with the Lord Jesus for ever and ever, when He comes with the trump of God.

When the believers are 'caught up' to be with the Lord, the dead shall be raised incorruptible and shall be changed in a moment in the twinkling of an eye. Then those, who have put on Christ, shall be 'caught up' together with them in the clouds to meet the Lord in the air and they will all be with the Lord for ever and ever.

Those, who did not believe in Jesus and did not
Leslie M. John

accept Him as their personal Savior miss these blessings of being 'caught up' and remain on this earth. The dead in sins will remain in their graves and the living will see with their eyes the Lord Jesus revealing Himself upon this earth.

The 'Son of man' will come with all the holy angels with him and shall sit upon the throne of glory. This prophesy was proclaimed in Zechariah 14th Chapter.

"And his feet shall stand in that day upon the mount of Olives, which is before Jerusalem on the east, and the mount of Olives shall cleave in the midst thereof toward the east and toward the west, and there shall be a very great valley; and half of the mountain shall remove toward the north and half of it toward the south". (Zechariah 14:4)

All nations (gentiles) will be gathered unto the Lord Jesus, when He sits on the throne of glory and He will separate one from the other just a shepherd divides his sheep from the goats.

The 'sheep' refers to the saved ones, who had their salvation during the period, when the Lord with His chaste bride is in the air, and likewise the 'goats' refers to the unsaved ones.

The King, who is our Lord and Savior Jesus Christ,

will then say unto those, who are on His right hand,
'Come, ye blessed of my Father' and then, the King,
who is our Lord and Savior Jesus Christ, will say
then say unto those, who are on his left hand,
'Depart from me, ye cursed, into everlasting fire,
prepared for devils and his angels'.

Leslie M. John

DEVOTIONAL 24
THE KING JUDGES

The words of the King at this judgment are very sharp and shrewd. To those, who are on His right hand, the King will say that when He was hungry they gave Him meat, and He was hungry they gave Him drink, and when he was a stranger, they took Him; Naked, and they clothed Him, and when He was sick they visited Him, when He was in prison, they went to see Him.

The righteous on the right side of the King will be filled with the surprise and ask the King, when He was hungry, thirsty, naked, sick and in prison. "And the King shall answer and say unto them, Verily I say unto you, Inasmuch as ye have done it unto one of the least of these my brethren, ye have done it unto me" (Matthew 25:40).

Similarly, the King, who is our Lord and Savior Jesus Christ will say very sharp and shrewd words to those, who are on His left side, that they did not give Him food when He was hungry, that they did not give him water when He was thirsty, that they did not take Him in when He was stranger, that they did not clothe him when He was naked, that they did not visit Him when He was sick, that they did not minister unto Him when He was in prison.

Leslie M. John

Those, whom the Word of God, calls as 'goats', (unsaved) ones, ask Him surprisingly, when they did not gave Him drink, food, and when was He naked that they did not clothe Him, and when was He stranger that they did not take Him in, and when He was sick that they did not minister unto Him, and when was in prison, that they did not minister unto Him.

"Then shall he answer them, saying, Verily I say unto you, Inasmuch as ye did it not to one of the least of these, ye did it not to me" (Matthew 25:45)

The blessings that the King shall give unto the righteous are that they will 'inherit the kingdom prepared for you from the foundation of the world' and the punishment the King renders unto those, who are not saved will be 'Depart from me, ye cursed, into everlasting fire, prepared for the devil and his angels'.

DEVOTIONAL 25
CONFORMED TO THE
IMAGE OF HIS SON

"Now therefore why tempt ye God, to put a yoke upon the neck of the disciples, which neither our fathers nor we were able to bear?" (Acts 15:10)

Who would want an inferior position that is earned through hard struggle when an exalted position is available easily? It is similar to this when Jews prefer to follow the Old Testament provisions while God has provided an easy method of procuring heavenly blessings through Lord Jesus Christ.

It is as simple as accepting Lord Jesus Christ as personal Savior by confessing sins to Him to receive glorified bodies at the twinkling of an eye when the 'Church' is 'caught up'. Those who will be caught up into mid-air to meet Lord Jesus Christ when He comes for His bride will be in the glorified bodies conformed to the image of Christ.

The Father gives to all those who are predestined to be confirmed to the image of His Son, glorified bodies, who rule with Him for a thousand years. All those who are left-behind and separated at the 'judgment of nations' to enter the 'kingdom' prepared for them will be in earthly bodies on this earth to be ruled over.

Leslie M. John

Lord Jesus Christ with His bride, the Church, the body of Christ, steps on to the Mount of olives and then after 'Sheep and Goat' judgment the Lord will rule over those who are on this earth.

The reign will be for thousand years. What a privilege is being lost by those who are called as "My People" by God that they are choosing to be on the earth with earthly bodies to be ruled over by Lord Jesus Christ and those that are confirmed to the image of Him.

"Blessed and holy is he that hath part in the first resurrection: on such the second death hath no power, but they shall be priests of God and of Christ, and shall reign with him a thousand years" (Revelation 20:6)

Leslie M. John

DEVOTIONAL 26
WAR AGIANST ANTICHRIST

"And I saw the beast, and the kings of the earth, and their armies, gathered together to make war against him that sat on the horse, and against his army" Revelation 19:19

At the second advent of our Lord Jesus Christ on this earth along with His 'bride' which is the "Church', the body of Christ, there shall accompany Him all the holy angels. Those that believed, Lord Jesus Christ as their Messiah, were 'caught up' to meet the Lord when He came with the sound of an archangel at the last trump. These are the ones who received the glorified bodies instantly at the twinkling of an eye. These are the ones who accompanied as army of the Lord along with the holy angels. (Ref: Revelation 19:11-18).

John also saw in his vision, as described in Revelation 19:19-21, Antichrist, kings of the earth, and their armies, gathered to make a war against Lord Jesus Christ, who sat on the horse, and against His army. Against Lord Jesus Christ and against those who accompanied Him were pitted the Antichrist, False prophets and the mighty kings of the earth.

Antichrist and the false prophets were taken alive

and cast into the 'lake of fire'. With the sword of
Lord Jesus Christ that proceeded from His mouth
were killed those entire remnant who became
feast to the fowls of the air.

"And the beast was taken, and with him the false
prophet that wrought miracles before him, with
which he deceived them that had received the
mark of the beast, and them that worshipped his
image. These both were cast alive into a lake of fire
burning with brimstone. And the remnant were
slain with the sword of him that sat upon the
horse, which [sword] proceeded out of his mouth:
and all the fowls were filled with their flesh" Rev
19:20-21.

DEVOTIONAL 27
THOUSAND YEAR REIGN OF LORD JESUS CHRIST

"And I saw an angel come down from heaven, having the key of the bottomless pit and a great chain in his hand". Revelation 20:1

John saw in his vision an angel coming down from heaven holding the key of the abyss and a huge chain in his hand. One fact that is very much noticeable here is that the angel coming down is not named.

The angel is neither Michael nor Gabriel. Satan is too inferior to the Father or the Son that the named powerful and mighty angels are not required to defeat him. It is enough that an unnamed angel is enough to bind Satan.

The Old Dragon, Satan, was already defeated at the cross and yet God has allowed him to be in the world with his limited power. Satan cannot do anything to any believer in Christ provided the believer depends on Lord Jesus Christ and has Him as rock of refuge. Otherwise, it will be like hitting hard a rock with a feeble fist.

The angel conquers Satan that cheated Eve and binds him and casts him into the abyss and shuts him up for thousand years in order that he may not cheat any one and then he puts a seal on the bottom-less pit where Satan will be bound. Satan will be let loose for a short period of time after the thousand-year-rule by Jesus Christ is completed.

John saw that there were thrones and judgment was given unto those who sat upon them. He saw the souls of martyrs of those who stood for Jesus and for the word of God. He also saw those who did not worship Antichrist, or his image, or received the mark of the beast either on their hands or on their foreheads. They all lived and reigned with Christ for thousand years.

"And I saw thrones, and they sat upon them, and judgment was given unto them: and [I saw] the souls of them that were beheaded for the witness of Jesus, and for the word of God, and which had not worshipped the beast, neither his image, neither had received [his] mark upon their foreheads, or in their hands; and they lived and reigned with Christ a thousand years. But the rest of the dead lived not again until the thousand years were finished. This [is] the first resurrection" Revelation 20:4-5

DEVOTIONAL 28
GREAT WHITE THRONE JUDGMENT

"Great White Throne Judgment is the final judgment and it is not to be confused with 'Judgment seat of Christ' or 'Sheep and Goat Judgment'

It is worth recalling about the judgments There are five judgments. The sequence is

(1) The Judgment at the cross (John 5:24)
(2) The Judgment in the mid-air for distribution of rewards for saints: (Also called as 'Bema seat of Christ'. (2 Cor. 5:10)
(3) The judgment of Jews and left-behind (Great Tribulation) - Matt 24:20-21
(4) The judgment of nations (also known as 'The Sheep and Goat Judgment) and
(5) The Judgment of the Wicked

"And I saw a great white throne, and him that sat on it, from whose face the earth and the heaven fled away; and there was found no place for them. And I saw the dead, small and great, stand before God; and the books were opened: and another book was opened, which is the book of life: and the dead were judged out of those things which were written in the books, according to their works.

Leslie M. John

83

(Revelation 20:11-12)" (Revelation 20:11)

All those who accept that the Son of God, Jesus, died for his/her sins, and accept him as the 'Lord' of one's life are saved from damnation. It is then that the soul dead in trespasses is redeemed; it is then that the soul is delivered from suffering the wrath of God. The soul that does not repent of his/her sins will be cast into lake of fire, by God, after the 'Great white throne judgment', which is the final judgment.

As and when our earthly house of this tabernacle gets dissolved we gain a building of God, the house not made with hands, but that which would be eternal in heavens. We groan in this body desiring to be clothed upon with the house that we would have in heavens, and that glorified body, which resurrects from the dead, when Jesus comes again, would not be naked; but the living soul with eternal life that does not marry nor is given in marriage. (Ref: 2 Cor. 5th Ch. Matthew 22:30 and Rom. 5th Ch.)

Apostle Peter reveals a marvelous truth in 1 Peter 1st Chapter. Addressing to the strangers scattered throughout Pontus, Galatia, Cappadocia, Asia and Bithynia he calls on Elect by God the Father, and wishes them 'Grace'.

All those, whom he addressed, were, as he says,

were begotten unto lively hope by the resurrection of Jesus Christ from the dead and to inherit incorruptible, and undefiled rewards that do not fade away.

These are reserved for them in heaven. These rewards are given to the believers in Christ in the mid-air when the Church is with the Lord. (Ref: 1 Thessalonians 4-16-17)

"For we must all appear before the judgment seat of Christ; that every one may receive the things done in his body, according to that he hath done, whether it be good or bad" (2 Corinthians 5:10)

DEVOTIONAL 29
JERUSALEM WILL BE CALLED BY A NEW NAME

The Holy city Jerusalem, the city of our Lord, is now desolate and not in good shape. The city is forsaken and destroyed. But, the day will come when the city will be called "Hephzibah", and its land "Beulah". The Lord delights in making the city delightful for every one and the land like married woman. (Isaiah Ch. 62:4). This is a prophecy about the status of Jerusalem in the millennial kingdom of Jesus.

Lord Jesus Christ is the Messiah. The Jews rejected him and called upon themselves the blood of Jesus in order that he may be crucified (Matthew 27:24-25). Peter's speech testifies about those who crucified Jesus.

"Ye men of Israel, hear these words; Jesus of Nazareth, a man approved of God among you by miracles and wonders and signs, which God did by him in the midst of you, as ye yourselves also know: Him, being delivered by the determinate counsel and foreknowledge of God, ye have taken, and by wicked hands have crucified and slain" (Acts 2:22-23)

Indeed, they paid the price in AD 70 according to

Leslie M. John

historians. Earlier, they worshipped idols many-a-time and were chastised by God. They rebelled against God and paid the price for their actions. Yet, they are His people; the city of David is His city and He will restore Israel to its past glory.

Like Boaz, who was kinsman redeemer of Ruth, Jesus is our redeemer. He came into this world, died for our sins, was buried, rose from the dead on the third day and later ascended into heaven. He is seated on the right hand of the Majesty and interceding for us. We, who are redeemed by the blood of Christ, are greater than the unrepentant Jews.

There is no condemnation for those, who have accepted Lord Jesus Christ as their personal savior, irrespective of their race, ethnicity, color, or creed. The Church consisting of saved ones stands above those Jews, who wait until 'Great Tribulation' to come to pass.

GENTILES SHALL SEE HIS RIGHTEOUSNESS

"And the Gentiles shall see thy righteousness, and all kings thy glory: and thou shalt be called by a new name, which the mouth of the LORD shall name" (Isaiah 62:2)
Lord Jesus Christ, who is the messiah, says that He will not sit quite, nor will He rest until He redeems the city of Jerusalem. He has set watchmen upon

the walls of Jerusalem and they will not keep quite nor will sleep but keep a watch over the city and will make the city a praise of the earth. This is a promise of Messiah and He has sworn by His right hand and by the arm of His strength. He promised that none of the enemies of Jerusalem will eat its corn as their food no stranger will ever drink its wine. Gentiles will see its righteousness.

Lord Jesus Christ defeats the kings loyal to Antichrist at 'Armageddon', and sits on the throne of David and reigns for a thousand years. In the thousand years of His rule there shall be perfect peace.

Satan will be bound with chains and thrown into abyss by an angel who comes from heaven. Later Satan will be released for a short time when he goes Gog and Magog to deceive the nations but fire from God comes down from heaven and devours Satan. (Revelation Ch. 20:8)

The dead who did not accept Jesus Christ as their personal savior will resurrect at that time. The Lord shall judge them at the 'Great white throne' and cast them along with death, hell, and the devil and his angels into the 'lake of fire' to be tormented for ever and ever.

This is the second death. For those who are saved, there is no second death but they will have everlasting life to be with the Lord for ever and ever. Note here when Antichrist and false prophet are thrown into the lake of fire! It is before the devil that deceived!!! Revelation 20:10 confirms it.

When the devil was cast into the lake of fire, the Antichrist and the false prophet were already there in the lake of fire. These are only the ones who will be in the lake of fire before the 'Great White Throne Judgment' (Revelation 16:16 and Revelation 20:8-10). Does the Scripture say any body is thrown into the lake of fire before Antichrist and false prophet? No, not at all!

There shall come out of heaven a New Jerusalem and we, who are saved, shall be in that Holy City. The Church is the bride of our Lord Jesus Christ and will be with Him for ever and ever reigning along with Him and every individual having been conformed to His image, irrespective of their earthly affiliation, while they were on the earth, to Jews or Gentiles.

DEVOTIONAL 30
STREET OF GOLD

"And the twelve gates were twelve pearls; every several gate was of one pearl: and the street of the city was pure gold, as it were transparent glass " (Revelation 21:21)

In this secular world we see the importance of gold. What if we who are common people in this world can tread on a street of gold, and live in a city made of the most precious metals?

Bible speaks of such precious metals, which even common man tread on, and live in a city made of most precious metals. Revelation chapter 21 presents the most beautiful city and the inhabitants there in.

John saw in his vision the holy city, New Jerusalem, coming down out of heaven from God, prepared for a bride, who was adorned for her husband. The description is great. Who is this bride? Bible speaks of the bride as the Church/Assembly constituting the believers in Christ, the saved ones.

The bride is adorned waiting for her husband to come and here is the chaste virgin, adorned waiting for the New Jerusalem. The tabernacle is

Leslie M. John

referred to in the Old Testament, as the sacred tent in which God came and dwelt. Here in this chapter John saw God himself coming down and dwelling among his people, who will be his people, and he will be their God, who will wipe away all their tears, and there will be no more death, nor sorrow, nor crying, no more pain, because all the old things have passed away by then.

It is the new heaven where the Assembly/Church, constituting the saved ones, which is his bride, will dwell.

Isaiah 65:17 presents the prophecy about the new heavens and a new earth that will be created and about the former earth and heaven which will pass away and will not be remembered.

In Revelation 21:1 we read that city, which is beautiful and which has no sea, but only the inhabitants, who are always happy and without any sufferings. Rev 21: 18 "And the building of the wall of it was of jasper: and the city was pure gold, like unto clear glass"

DEVOTIONAL 31
OUR ABODE FOR EVER AND EVER

Our savior Jesus Christ has undergone severe pain when men pierced sword in to his body and beat him. He was crowned with a crown of thorns and blood and water gushed forth from the side of his body. It is through that blood of Jesus Christ that we are saved. He suffered on the cross of Calvary that so that we may have eternal life.

It is through the shedding of his precious blood that our sins are cleansed and through that blood of Christ that our filth is cleansed and we are made clear as crystal. That city of precious metals is prepared for us.

But for those who do not accept Jesus Christ as their personal Savior, there is another place designated and it is the lake of fire, as we read in Rev. 21: 8. It is described as the "lake which burneth with fire and brimstone" which is the second death.

"And I saw no temple therein: for the Lord God Almighty and the Lamb are the temple of it. And the city had no need of the sun, neither of the moon, to shine in it: for the glory of God did lighten it, and the Lamb is the light thereof"
In the beginning God called light into existence and

Leslie M. John

He saw that the light was good and God divided light from darkness.

"And God saw the light, that it was good: and God divided the light from the darkness. And God called the light Day, and the darkness he called Night. And the evening and the morning were the first day" (Genesis 1:4-5)

On the fourth day of creation God made two great lights - the greater to rule the day and the lesser to rule the night and He made stars also. We know them by 'sun' and 'moon'. These two lights were created to divide day from night and let them be for signs and for seasons and for days and years. In eternity we do not need such divisions.

New Jerusalem where we dwell does not need sun and moon to shine in it because the glory of God that shines in it is greater than any light. The Lamb of God, who is our Lord Jesus Christ, is the light in it.

"And God said, Let there be lights in the firmament of the heaven to divide the day from the night; and let them be for signs, and for seasons, and for days, and years" (Genesis 1:14)

"And the city had no need of the sun, neither of the moon, to shine in it: for the glory of God did lighten it, and the Lamb is the light thereof" (Revelation

21:23)

"And there shall be no night there; and they need no candle, neither light of the sun; for the Lord God giveth them light: and they shall reign for ever and ever" (Revelation 22:5)

.

.